P9-CLC-444

THEMATIC UNIT
Animals

Written by Janet Hale

Illustrated by Blanca Apodaca, Paula Spence, and Sue Fullam

Teacher Created Materials, Inc.
P. O. Box 1214
Huntington Beach, CA 92647
© *1990 Teacher Created Materials, Inc.*
Made in U. S. A.

ISBN–1–55734–250–4

The classroom teacher may reproduce copies of materials in this book for classroom use only. The reproduction of any part for an entire school or school system is strictly prohibited. No part of this publication may be transmitted, stored, or recorded in any form without written permission from the publisher.

Table of Contents

INTRODUCTION **3**

FARM ANIMALS **5**

Nature's Footprints: In the Barnyard by Q.L. and W.J. Pearce (Silver Press, 1990)

    Summary—Suggested Activities—Activity Pages—Animal Poems

CIRCUS ANIMALS **24**

Spot Goes to the Circus by Eric Hill (Putnam, 1986)

    Summary—Suggested Activities—Activity Pages—Audio - Visual Ideas

ZOO ANIMALS **39**

Dear Zoo by Rod Campbell (Penguin, 1987)

    Summary—Suggested Activities—Activity Pages—Zoo Field Trip Notice

PETS **57**

The Pop-Up Pet Shop by Rod Campbell (Macmillan, 1989)

    Summary—Suggested Activities—Activity Pages—Stuffed Animal Day Notice—General Animal Activities

UNIT MANAGEMENT **72**

    Recipes—Bulletin Board

BIBLIOGRAPHY **80**

Introduction

Animals contains four captivating whole language, thematic units: **Farm**, **Circus**, **Zoo**, and **Pets**. Its 80 exciting pages are filled with a wide variety of lesson ideas and activities designed for use with children at the early childhood level. Each unit has at its core a high-quality children's literature selection: Farm — *In the Barnyard*; Circus — *Spot Goes to the Circus*; Zoo — *Dear Zoo*; and Pets — *The Pop-Up Pet Shop*. For each of these books, activities are included which set the stage for reading, encourage the enjoyment of the book, and extend the concepts gained. In addition, the theme is connected to the curriculum with activities in language arts (including language experience and writing suggestions), math, science, social studies, art, music, and life skills (cooking, physical education, etc.) Many of these activities encourage cooperative learning. Suggestions and patterns for bulletin boards are additional time savers for the busy teacher. Futhermore, directions for student-created Big Books and culminating activities, which allow students to synthesize their knowledge in order to produce products that can be shared beyond the classroom, highlight this very complete teacher resource.

This thematic unit includes:

☐ **literature selections** — summaries of four children's books with related lessons (complete with reproducible pages) that cross the curriculum

☐ **poetry** — suggested selections and lessons enabling students to write and publish their own works.

☐ **language experience and writing ideas** — daily suggestions as well as activities across the curriculum, including Big Books

☐ **bulletin board ideas** — suggestions and plans for student-created and/or interactive bulletin boards

☐ **homework suggestions** — extending the unit to the child's home

☐ **curriculum connections** — in language arts, math, science, social studies, art, music, and life skills such as cooking, and physical education

☐ **group projects** — to foster cooperative learning

☐ **culminating activities** — which require students to synthesize their learning to produce a product or engage in an activity that can be shared with others

☐ **a bibliography** — suggesting additional literature and nonfiction books on the theme

---

To keep this valuable resource intact so it can be used year after year, you may wish to punch holes in the pages and store them in a three-ring binder.

Introduction (cont.)

Why Whole Language?

A whole language approach involves children in using all modes of communication: reading, writing, listening, observing, illustrating, experiencing, and doing. Communication skills are interconnected and integrated into lessons that emphasize the whole of language rather than isolating its parts. The lessons revolve around selected literature. Reading is not taught as a separate subject from writing and spelling, for example. A child reads, writes (spelling appropriately for his/her level), speaks, listens, etc. in response to a literature experience introduced by the teacher. In this way, language skills grow naturally, stimulated by involvement and interest in the topic at hand.

Why Thematic Planning?

One very useful tool for implementing an integrated whole language program is thematic planning. By choosing a theme with correlating literature selections for a unit of study, a teacher can plan activities throughout the day that lead to a cohesive, in-depth study of the topic. Students will be practicing and applying their skills in meaningful contexts. Consequently, they will tend to learn and retain more. Both teachers and students will be freed from a day that is broken into unrelated segments of isolated drill and practice.

Why Cooperative Learning?

Besides academic skills and content, students need to learn social skills. No longer can this area of development be taken for granted. Students must learn to work cooperatively in groups in order to function well in modern society. Group activities should be a regular part of school life and teachers should consciously include social objectives as well as academic objectives in their planning. For example, a group working together to write a report may need to select a leader. The teacher should make clear to the students and monitor the qualities of good leader-follower group interaction just as he/she would state and monitor the academic goals of the project.

Why Big Books?

An excellent cooperative, whole language activity is the production of Big Books. Groups of students, or the whole class, can apply their language skills, content knowledge, and creativity to produce a Big Book that can become a part of the classroom library to be read and reread. These books make excellent culminating projects for sharing beyond the classroom with parents, librarians, other classes, etc. Big Books can be produced in many ways and this thematic unit book includes directions for at least one method you may choose.

Farm Animals

Nature's Footprints: In the Barnyard

By Q.L. Pearce and W.J. Pearce

Summary

In The Barnyard combines the introduction of ten farm animals with the sounds, footprints and products they produce. To encourage higher level thinking skills, students are directed to identify the animal's footprints and follow them on a two-page mural.

Suggested Activities

Concepts

A. Animals live in families.
B. Each family member has a name.
C. We use products made by/from animals.

Concept Activities

Farm Animal Families

Using pictures, introduce farm animals by emphasizing the name of each family member. Discuss the size, shape, and color of each family member. Fill in a graph to show which animals are tall, short, fat, thin, etc. How many legs, eyes, ears, and other body parts does each animal have?

Classify all of the male, female, and baby family names on chart paper. Have students draw pictures and display around chart.

Chickens: **Rooster, Hen, Chicks**   *Horses:* **Stallion, Mare, Foal (Colt=boy, Filly=girl)**
Pigs: **Boar, Sow, Calf**   *Goats:* **Billy Goat, Nanny, Kid**
Sheep: **Ram, Ewe, Lamb**   *Ducks:* **Drake, Duck, Duckling**

Farm Animal Products

Bring in a "product" for each farm animal. Allow students to touch or taste and talk about each product. Make a variety of graphs showing likes/dislikes, colors, texture, and uses of each product.

Edible Products:

Eggs, Meat=Chicken, Turkey
Milk, Cheese, Beef=Cow
Bacon, Ham, Sausage=Pig
Milk, Cheese=Goat

Usable Products:

Feathers (Down)= Geese
Leather for Boots, Belts=Cow
Wool= Sheep

Other Ways Animals Help:

Catches mice= Cat
Herds cattle, protects farmer and farm= Dogs
Pulls equipment= Horse, Mule, Donkey

Take the class on a field trip to a major grocery store to see the products on the shelves. Take pictures of the farm animals and have students classify the correct animal with the correct products.

Suggested Activities *(cont.)*

Additional Farm Animal Activities

Farm Animal Sounds

1. Reread the story, having students repeat the animals' sounds after you initially read them.

2. Play a pre-recorded tape of the ten animals sounds (in a mixed order). Have students call out the animal's name when they hear the sound it makes.

3. Play a Farm Animal Sounds game by using the concept of Simon Says: "Farmer Simon says...make a sound like a pig...."

Farm Animal Footprints

1. Review the book by showing the set of footprints for each farm animal. Then show footprint cards (pages 9 and 10). Have students guess which animal's footprints you are holding. Refer back to the book to verify the answers.

2. Compare the animals' footprints. Whose are alike? Different?

3. Make enough copies of the various footprint cards (pages 9 and 10) to create a "path." For practicing gross motor skills, have students follow the paths around the classroom or outside. For added fun, have students also say the appropriate animal's sound! To enrich oral language, have pathways go under, over, through, around, between, and beside objects. Discuss these words in detail as the children are following the paths.

4. Discuss that we (humans) also make footprints. If a sandbox is available, allow students to make their footprints in the sand. Trace students' feet to make human footprints and use them to reinforce skills being taught by writing information onto each print (e.g., numbers 0–10, ABC's). Lay out in a path. Allow students to follow the path and say the number, letter, or sight word on each print as they are following the pathway.

6 © 1990 Teacher Created Materials, Inc.

Suggested Activities *(cont.)*

More Farm Animal Activities

- Make a mural of a barnyard; include the silo, barn, pens, farmhouse, well, etc.. Discuss the farm items and how they are helpful to the farmer and/or animals. Using paint, markers, chalk, or crayons, each student should draw their favorite farm animal. Cut out and staple onto the background mural.

- Invite a farmer to the classroom and have him talk about caring for farm animals. Maybe he can bring in a live animal or two!
- Incubate chicken eggs in an incubator. It takes 21 days for the chicken eggs to hatch. Make sure that you can fulfill all the requirements for hatching the chicks! A local farmer, chicken rancher, 4-H club, or science center can help you!

- Visit a farm for a field trip experience.
- For improving fine motor skills use the lace cards on page 11 and 12.
- Bring in a wool sweater. Allow the students to feel it. Describe how it feels. Complete page 13 together.

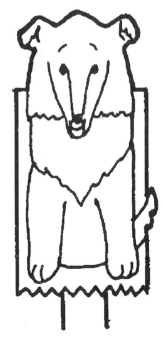

- Make the dog puppet on pages 15 and 16. Have students practice oral speaking skills by having them tell you about the farm animals by pretending they are the farm dog and speaking to you!
- Make Farm Scene Sandwiches (page 72).
- Read supplemental resources about animals or life on a farm. Write a class rhyming poem about a farm animal.

Example:

There was a red hen,

She lived in a pen,

She planted some wheat,

And made a tasty wheat treat!

Culminating Activities

1. Review the book, *In The Barnyard,* having students say the animal sounds. Teach or review the traditional "Old McDonald Had a Farm" song. Clean out an empty half gallon milk carton. Place farm animal pictures inside. (You may wish to use the picture cards on pages 21-23.) Place on a table. Ask a student to reach in and pull out a small picture of a farm animal. Have the class identify the animal and sing "Old McDonald" using that particular animal's sound.

2. Review the concept that farms are filled with different kinds of animals. Make one or more of the farm scene to be used for group/individual activities (pages 20-23). Reproduce pieces; you may wish to use heavy paper. The assembling of pieces can be done in small groups with parental aid or as an entire class. After all pieces have been colored, cut out, and folded to stand up, they can be laminated for extra support to be used again later. Below are some ideas that can be used with the created farm scenes:

   - Write a class story about a day on the farm.
   - Have students create a small "puppet" play using the farm scene pieces. Allow them to present their plays to each other.
   - Sing "Old McDonald Had a Farm," but this time have students hold up the animal that they are singing about.
   - Staple the cards together on the left edge to create a visual Farm Animal Book.
   - Count the animals on each piece and stand them up in order from the most animals to the least. Classify the animals with the same number of legs.
   - Ask another class to come in and pair up a student from your room with one from the other. Allow the teams of two to play with the farm scene together. Encourage your students to share the information they have learned about farm animals with their special guest!

8   © 1990 Teacher Created Materials, Inc.

Animal Footprint Cards
(Cut apart)

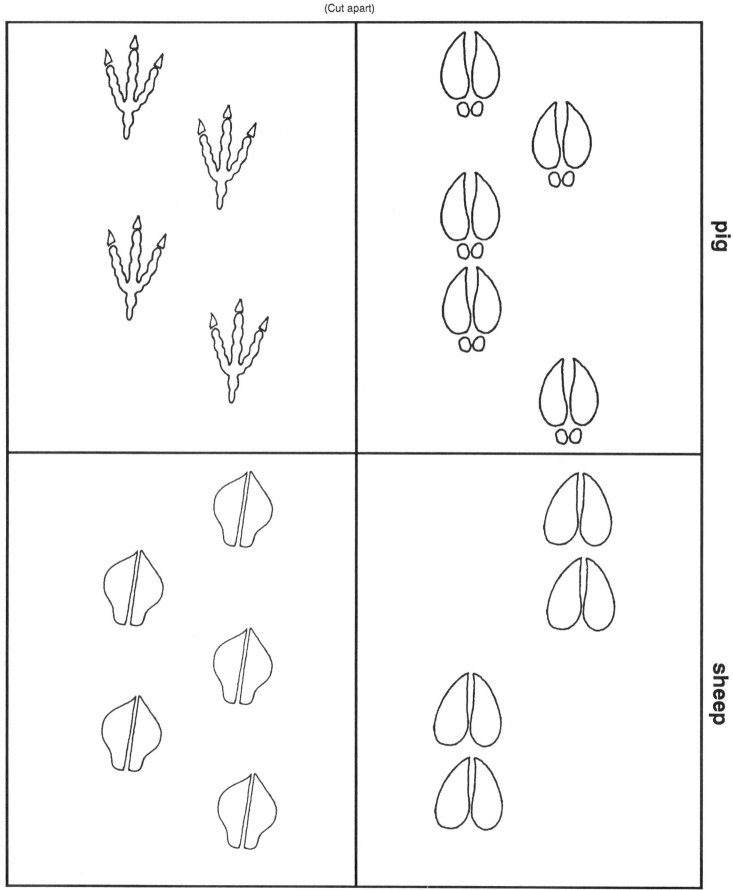

pig

sheep

Animal Footprint Cards

(Cut apart)

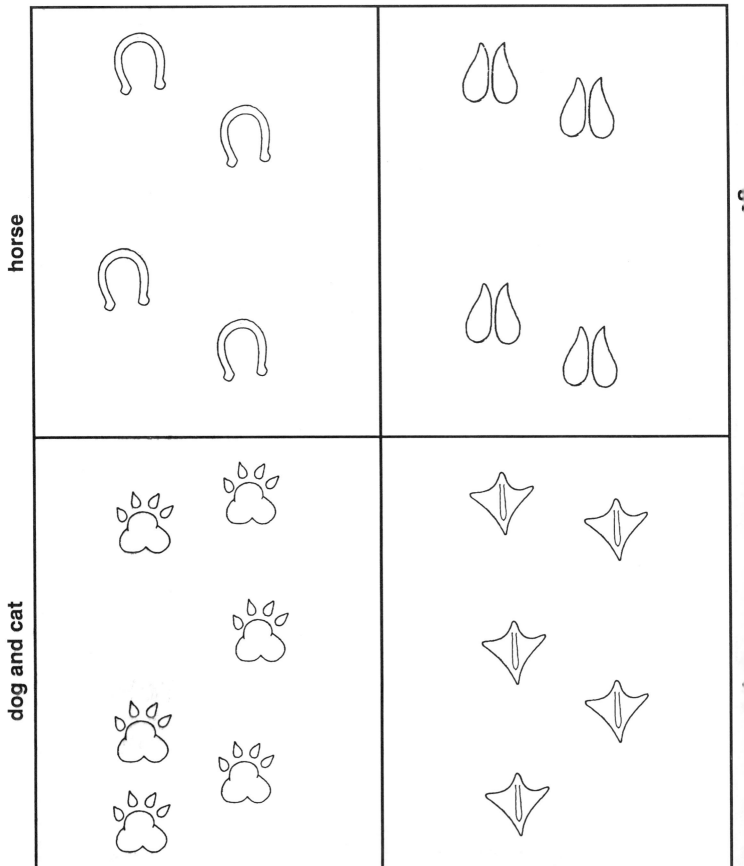

Lace Cards

Cut out each card and glue individually onto oak tag. Punch out holes with a one hole pu.
yarn pieces with tape or use a shoe string. Tie a knot at one end of yarn, pull through one h.
remaining cards. Place in center or free time area.

pig

duck

© 1990 Teacher Created Materials, Inc.

Lace Cards *(cont.)*

chicken

© 1990 Teacher Created Materials, Inc.

1. Color sheep's face and legs.
2. Glue cotton balls to sheep's body.

We get wool from sheep

Sheep

Farm Animals

Color the animals that are alike.

Dog Puppet

1. Color pages 15 and 16.

2. Cut out.

3. Glue to top of paper bag.

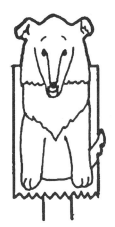

*See suggested activity page 7.

© 1990 Teacher Created Materials, Inc.   15

Dog Puppet *(cont.)*

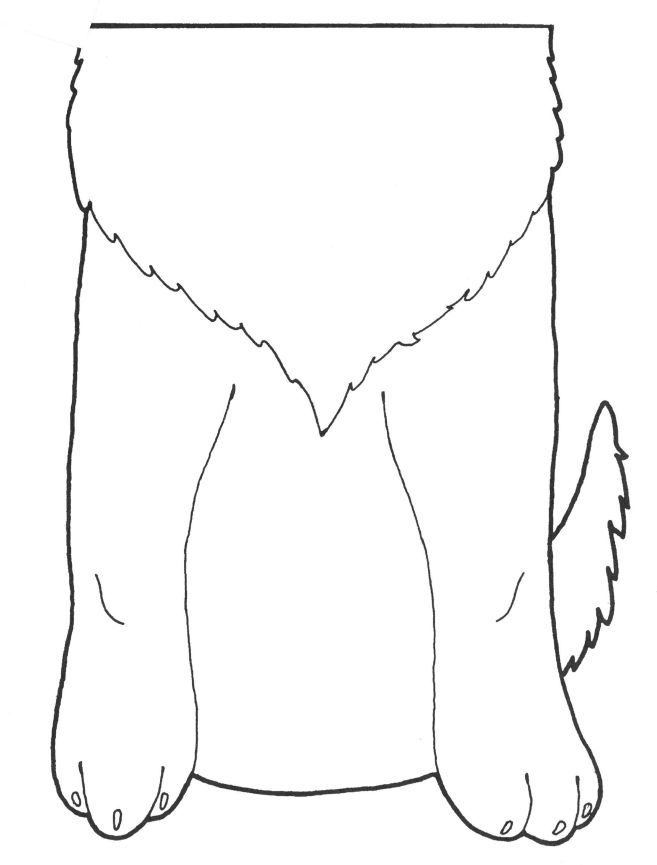

16

© 1990 Teacher Created Materials, Inc.

Name _____

The Rooster

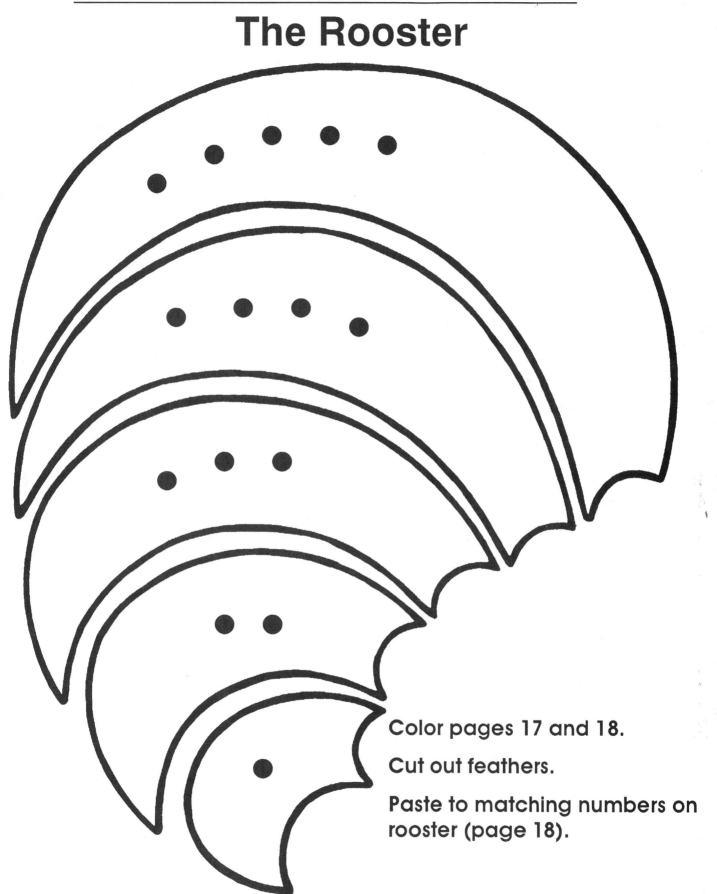

Color pages 17 and 18.

Cut out feathers.

Paste to matching numbers on rooster (page 18).

The rooster wakes up the farmer.

Animal Poems

Goose Feathers

Cackle, Cackle, Mother Goose,

Have you any feathers loose?

Truly have I, pretty fellow,

Half enough to fill a pillow.

Here are quills, take one or two,

And down to make a bed for you!

A Pig

A pig loves the mud, it helps him stay cool,

Since he can't sweat, or swim in a pool!

Bow-Wow

Bow-wow says the dog,

Mew, mew says the cat,

Grunt, grunt goes the hog,

And squeak goes the rat.

Whoo-oo says the owl,

Caw, caw says the crow,

Quack, quack says the duck,

And what cuckoos say, you know.

So with cuckoos and owls,

With rats and with dogs,

With ducks and with crows,

With cats and with hogs,

A fine song I have made,

To please you, my dear;

And if it's well-sung,

"Twill be charming to hear!

The Black Hen

Hickety, pickety, my black hen,

She lays eggs for gentlemen;

Gentlemen come every day

To see what my black hen does lay!

Baa, Baa, Black Sheep

Baa, Baa, black sheep, have you any wool?

Yes, sir; yes, sir; three bags full.

One for the master, one for the dame,

And one for the little boy who lives down the lane!

Farm Animal Scene

Color and cut out pieces on pages 20–23.

*See page 8 for suggested activities.

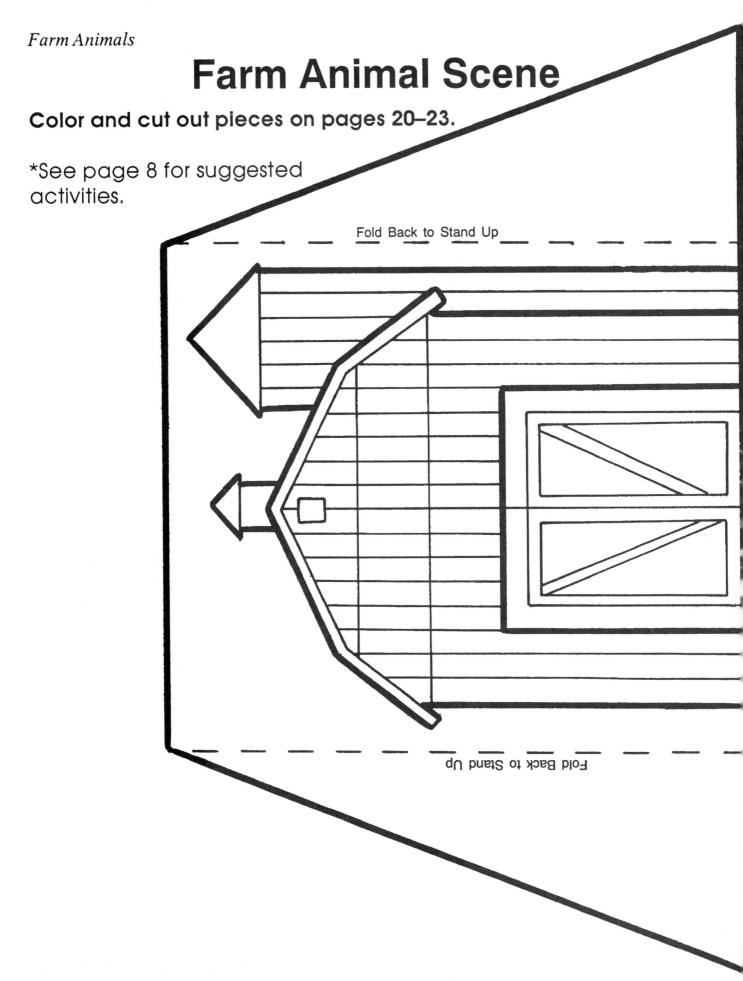

Fold Back to Stand Up

Fold Back to Stand Up

© *1990 Teacher Created Materials, Inc.*

Farm Animal Scene *(cont.)*

Fold back on dotted lines so card will stand up.

Farm Animal Scene *(cont.)*

Fold back on dotted lines so card will stand up.

Farm Animal Scene *(cont.)*

Fold back on dotted lines so card will stand up.

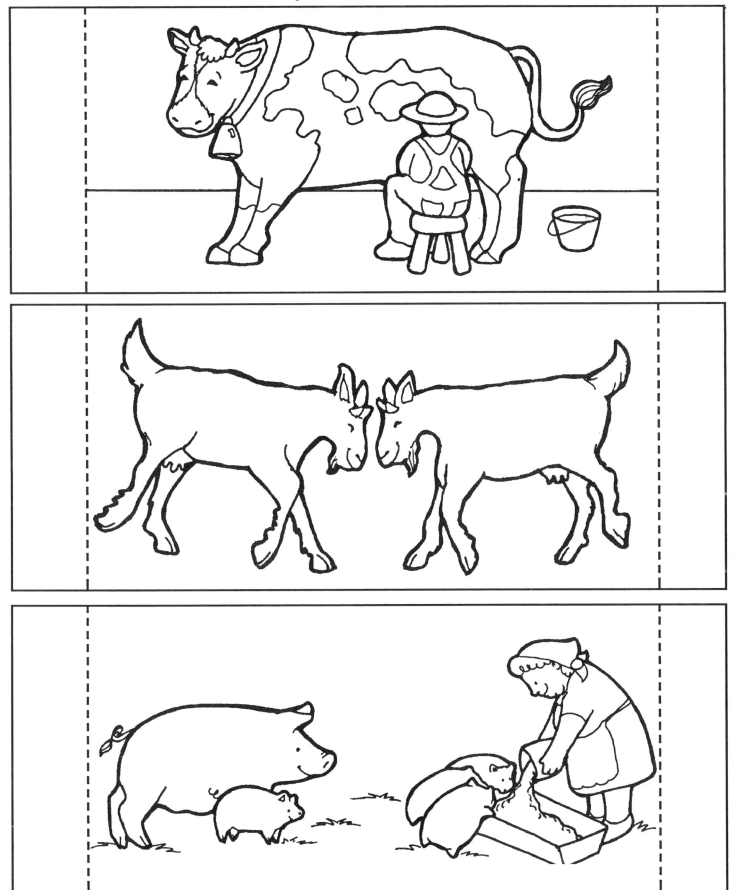

Circus Animals

Spot Goes to the Circus
By Eric Hill
Summary

Spot goes on an adventure through the circus in search of his lost ball. He meets various animals performing tricks along the way. He asks them if they have seen his ball and their reply is found hidden behind a flap. Finally, he finds the seal with this ball and not only makes a new friend, but learns a circus trick, too!

Suggested Activities

Concepts

A. Animals have body parts.
B. Some animals are trained to perform tricks.
C. Animals use different body parts to help them perform the tricks.

Concept Activities

Circus Animal Body Parts

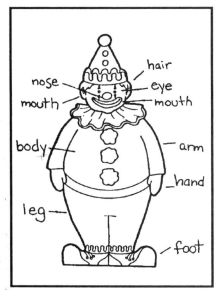

Introduce and/or review human body parts by playing Simple Simon. Ask, "What parts of our body do we use to complete a task (job)?" ***Examples:*** **Hands=** hold a broom, brush our hair; **Legs=** walk, jump, sit cross-legged

Show a picture of a circus clown. (Enlarge clown on page 28.) Label body parts. Display.

Show a picture of each animal Spot meets. Discuss the body parts of each animal. Make a graph to show which animals Spot meets have the same body parts. Look back at the story. Which body parts did each animal use to perform its trick?

Extension: Compare circus animal body parts to farm animal body parts.

	flippers	4 legs	2 legs	2 arms	head	neck	tail	body	nose	foot	hoof	hand	paw	ears	eyes	whiskers
Elephant		■			■	■	■	■	■	■				■	■	
Tiger		■			■	■	■	■	■				■	■	■	■
Kangaroo			■	■	■	■	■	■	■	■		■		■	■	
Lion		■			■	■	■	■	■				■	■	■	■
Bear		■			■	■	■	■	■	■			■	■	■	
Pig		■			■		■	■	■		■			■	■	
Monkey			■	■	■	■	■	■	■			■		■	■	
Seal	■				■	■	■	■	■						■	■

© 1990 Teacher Created Materials, Inc.

Suggested Activities *(cont.)*

Circus Animal Tricks

Explain that circus animals have owners that take care of them. They are called trainers. The trainers also train the animals to perform (learn and do) tricks. The trainer is the animal's "teacher." Just like students learn in steps, animals learn their tricks in steps, too. The steps are:

1. Get the animal used to people.
   (How do you feel around people you don't know?)

2. Give the animal a tasty treat.
   (What is your favorite treat?)

3. Show the animal how to do a trick.
   (Think about how you learned to ride a tricycle... what steps did it take to learn?)

4. When the animal tries the shown trick, and does it right, he gets his favorite treat!

Teach the students how to do a "trick."

1. Give each student a handshake.

2. Show a treat to the class.

3. Demonstrate the trick. (Hop on one foot.)

4. Have students "perform" trick and "reward" with treat!

5. Explain that if the trainer always gave the animal a food treat the animal would get very fat! Instead the trainers sometimes just give a "love clap" or a "love tap," which tells the animal that the trainer is proud of the trick they performed.

6. Continue with another "trick," but this time give the students a round of applause instead of a treat. Ask what body parts they used to perform the trick.

If students are old enough, divide into teams of two. (An alternative is a parent-helper or aide working with one or two students.) Have each student take a turn being the trainer and training their "animal." They can give "love claps" for a reward, too!

Possible Tricks:

catch a ball	**jump on two feet**	**run in place**
walk a straight line	**balance on one leg**	**balance a book on head**

Suggested Activities *(cont.)*

Circus Animal Activities

A Three Ring Act

Use chalk or masking tape to place three large rings on the classroom floor or blacktop outside. Have the students perform "tricks" (calisthenics) in each ring. To add variety, have students pretend they are the various animals found in the circus and encourage them to make the appropriate animal sounds. Oral language can also be practiced by asking students to go in, out, beside, on, near, next to, below, above, to the right, to the left, and through one, two, or all three of the circles.

Circus Performers Mural

Review the book, emphasizing the tricks and body parts used by each animal. Make a "three ring" circus mural. Provide paper and allow students to draw a picture of an animal performing a trick. Before placing the picture on the mural, have the student tell you what part(s) of the animal's body it uses to perform the trick.

Circus Field Trip

Go to the circus if it comes to town! Arrange a behind-the-scenes tour and meet the trainers and their performing animals!

What Is It?

Show students pictures of animals and people. Compare their body parts. Which animals have the same/different body parts as people? Have students cover their eyes while the teacher covers up a body part on a picture of an animal or person. Students then look and call out the body part that has been covered up. As each body part is identified, label the body part with a marking pen. Have students lie on large pieces of butcher paper. Trace around their bodies. Allow them to color their bodies to look like themselves. Use the labeled pictures as a reference so they can label their own body. Display the finished, labeled bodies in the classroom or hallway.

 © 1990 Teacher Created Materials, Inc.

Suggested Activities *(cont.)*

More Circus Animal Activities

- **Word Match:** Reproduce page 31 on heavy paper to help students learn to identify and spell a few of the circus animal names they have been learning about. Cut the pictures from the words. Mix and match. The activity can be done in small groups, at a learning center, or as a class.

- **Elephant Treat:** An elephant's favorite treat when he performs a trick is peanuts. Provide each student with ten peanuts (in shells). Play counting games with the peanuts. Hand out page 32 and have students complete. When students have had their answers checked (and corrected, if necessary), allow them to eat their peanuts as a special treat!

- **A Classifying Tent:** Using pages 33 and 34, have students classify the animals into the correct circus ring.

- **A Balancing Act:** Follow the directions to play the Balancing Balloon Race on page 35. This activity is designed to encourage the use of gross and fine motor skills.

- **Animal Cookies:** As a reward for positive classroom behaviors, as an incentive, or for a fun treat, present animal cookies in small circus boxes. Animal cookies can be found in drug or grocery stores.).

- **Story Time:** Use the additional reading resources (page 80) and/or general animal activities (page 71) to extend lessons taught.

Culminating Activity

A Circus Animal Book

Provide a copy of page 37 for each student. Have them dictate or write the name of their favorite circus animal. Allow them to draw a picture of their animal performing a trick. Ask them to tell you what body parts their animal used to perform the trick. Collect all of the pages. Place a sturdy cover page made from colored paper on the top and tie together with a string on the left side. Entitle the cover with "Our Class Circus Book." Read the book to the class. Place it in a free time or reading center area for all to review and enjoy!

27

A Circus Clown

*See suggested activity
page 24.

Name_____

A Trick

Color, cut, and paste.

© 1990 Teacher Created Materials, Inc.

250 Thematic Unit — Animals

Circus Animals

Guess Who?

Name _____

Connect the dots. Color.

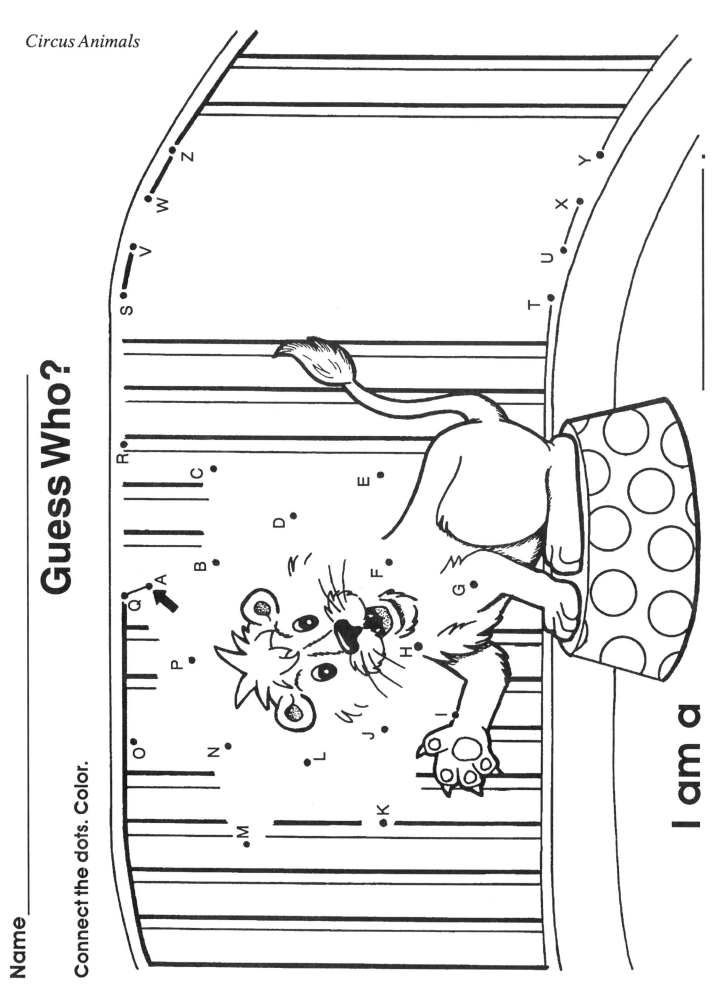

I am a _____

Name_____

Circus Animals

*See suggested activity, page 27.

	tiger
	kangaroo
	lion
	bear
	seal

Feed the Elephants

Draw a line from each peanut to the matching elephant. Color.

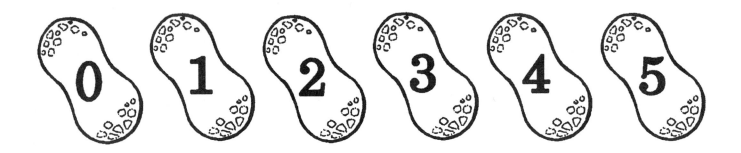

Elephants can do tricks for peanuts.

Three Ring Circus

1. Color the animals doing tricks.
2. Count the animals in each group.
3. Cut and match the animals to the 3 rings (page 34).
4. Glue.

Circus Animals

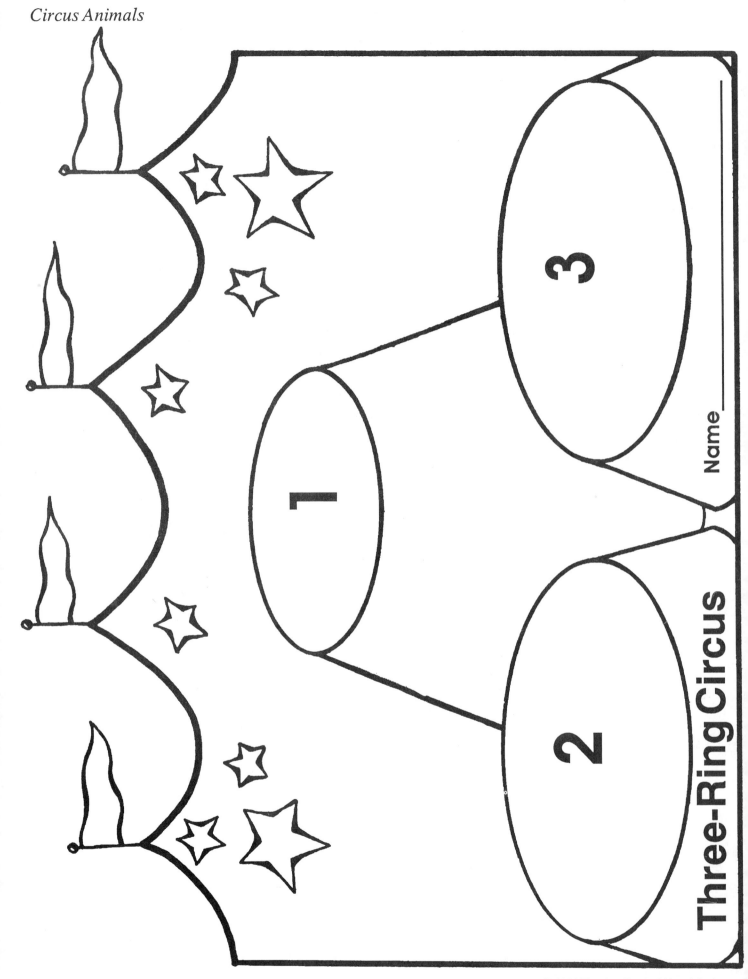

Name _____

Three-Ring Circus

34

© 1990 Teacher Created Materials, Inc.

Balancing Balloon Race

Balancing a ball is a real trick! Seals can make it look easy!
Give your class a chance at balancing a balloon in this fun race!

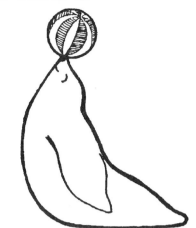

Equipment

Chalk or masking tape, 1 plastic spoon per team, 1 blown-up
balloon per student, large container (box, barrel, basket) (one
per team), large indoor or outdoor play area

Directions

1. Using masking tape or chalk, draw a starting line.

2. Divide the class into equal teams. (There may be more than 2 teams.)

3. Line teams up behind the starting line. Have students sit down.

4. Place containers at opposite end of play area, one per team.

5. Give a balloon to each child.

6. Give the first child on each team a plastic spoon.

7. Explain that when you say go, the first child is to walk as fast as possible, balancing the balloon on the
   spoon, until he gets to the container, drops the balloon in and walks back to his team, passing the spoon
   to the next player.

8. The winners can be determined in two ways:

   a. The team that gets all of their balloons into the container first.

   b. The team that gets the most balloons in the container in a given amount of time.

Circus Animals

Help Spot get to the circus.

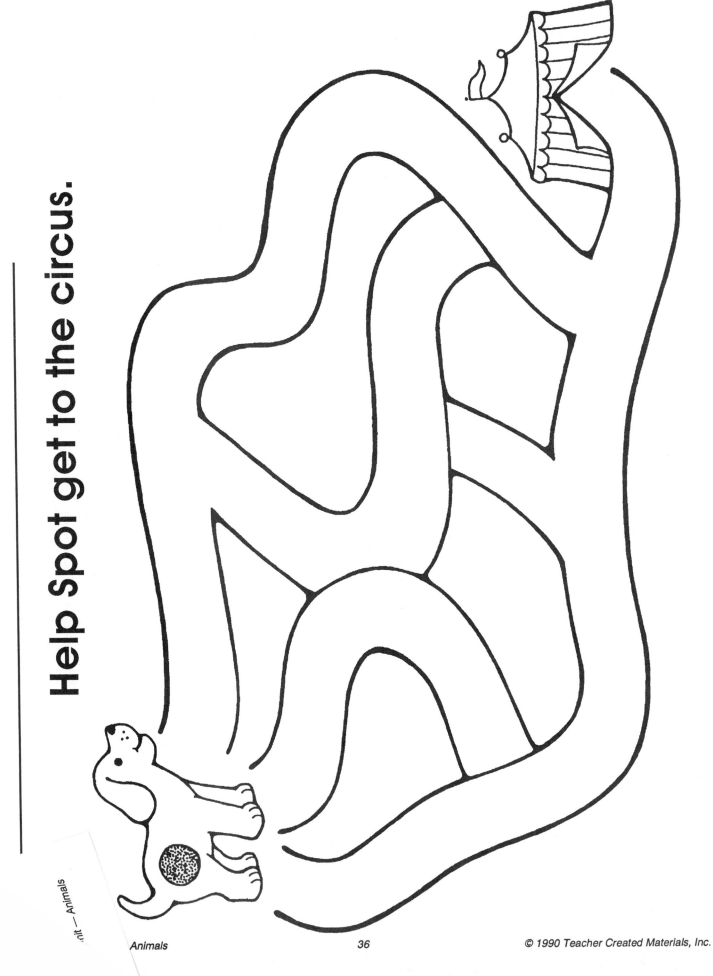

© 1990 Teacher Created Materials, Inc.

My Favorite Circus Animal

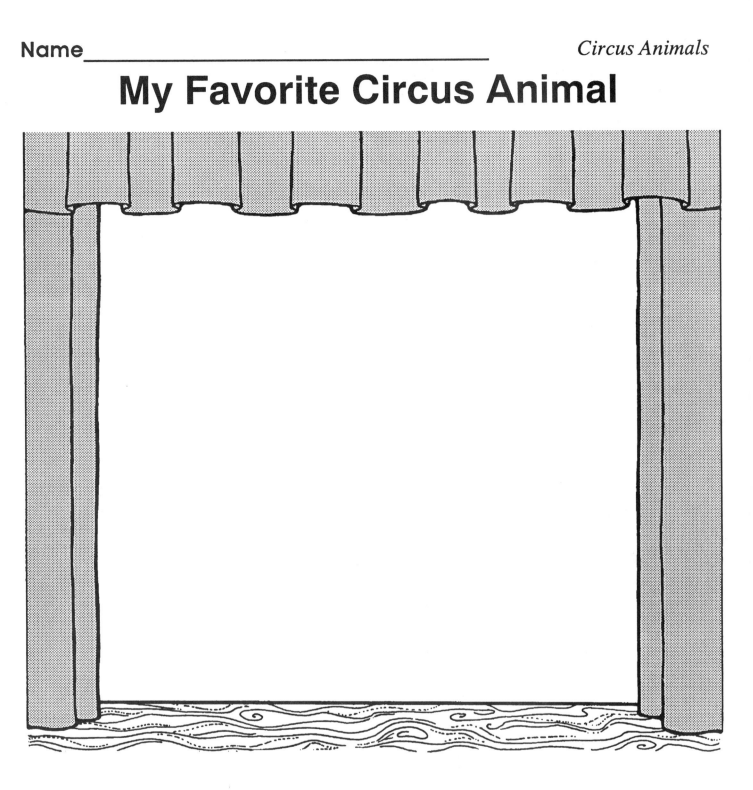

My favorite circus animal is a

_____.

Animal Audio-Visual Ideas

During each day of your animal thematic unit show one of the filmstrips or movies listed. Your library or resource office may have alternatives.

Have students make their own taped story about animals. Record their thoughts and ideas. Place the finished tape in a center or free-time area.

Look at the monthly programming on public television stations. Often they will give an outline of up-coming shows. Try to arrange a time for your class to view a special animal program.

Have students from the upper grades come to your classroom and read animal stories to the class. Encourage open discussion at the end of each story reading time.

Filmstrips

Finding Out How Animal Babies Grow
Farm Animals
Pets

All Available through:
SVE (Society for Visual Education, Inc.)
Dept. JP
1345 Diversey Parkway
Chicago, Ill. 60614-1299

16 mm Films

Zoo Baby Animals
Farm Animals
Elephants
The Zoo
Pigs

Cows

Available through:
EBE (Encyclopedia Britannica Educational Films)
425 N. Michigan Avenue
Chicago, Ill 60611

Churchill Films
12210 Nebraska Avenue
Los Angeles, CA 90025

Chickens
Dogs, Dogs, Dogs

AIMS
6901 Woodley Avenue
Van Nuys, CA 91406-4878

38 *© 1990 Teacher Created Materials, Inc.*

Zoo Animals

Dear Zoo
By Rod Campbell
Summary

Dear Zoo is a delightful way of encountering zoo animals for a first-time experience in hypothesizing. Each animal is sent to a child who has asked for a pet from the zoo. Using visual clues (the container in which the animal comes) and the written text, the students are asked to "guess" what has been sent before the container is "opened." The story contains excellent oral language and visual discrimination opportunities.

Note: As you initially read this story to the class, encourage hypothesizing before revealing the true identity of each animal!

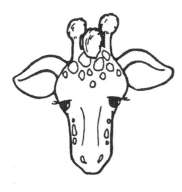

Suggested Activities

Concepts

A. Animals live in different habitats.

B. Animals eat different kinds of food.

Concept Activities

Zoo Animal Homes

Review the story and ask the students to notice the different containers that the animals came in. Were they short, tall, round, square? Ask if the animals always live in these containers.

Explain that where an animal lives is called its habitat. In old zoos they used to keep all of the animals in cages, but the animals were very unhappy because a cage was not like their real habitat (home). Ask if any of the students would like to live in a little box all day, everyday! Explain that zoos today are very careful about the animals' homes. They make sure that the animals in the zoo are living in their special habitat. Using some of the additional reading resources (page 80), read about the different animals and their habitats. A chart on the next page has been developed to provide the teacher with a handy resource to use when giving students details during animal discussions. Discuss the different habitats. Compare and classify the animals that live in the same habitats. Show the class a globe. Locate Africa and explain that many zoo animals can be found in Africa. Point out on the globe where students live. Explain that we live far away from Africa. Since it is so far away, the zoo is a special place where we can go and see these animals.

	Land Region	Food It Eats	Actual "Home"
ant	grasslands	grass, bamboo, roots, water plants	open range
Giraffe	grasslands woodlands	leaves, twigs, fruit, berries	open range
Lion	grasslands	meat	open range, in dens
Camel	desert	leaves, hay, dates, grass, grains	open desert
Snake	desert, forests	rodents	trees, burrows, under brush
Monkey	tropical forests	leaves, stem, bark, fruit, roots	trees
Frog	tropical forests deserts, ponds	insects, worms, spiders, minnows	water, burrows, under rocks

Other animals live in these land regions:

Grasslands: Zebras, Hippos, Ostriches, Rhinos
Temperate Forests: Beavers, Bears, Moose, Deer, Otters
Tropical Forests: Gorillas, Jaguars, Tapirs, Deer, Macaws
Desert: Dingos, Foxes, Lizards, Coyotes, Gila Monsters, Owls, Bats
Polar: Polar Bears, Brown Bears, Walruses, Penguins, Musk Oxen

Classify the animals by their habitat regions onto large butcher paper backgrounds. Find pictures or have students draw their own animals. As you discuss each region use expressive language to describe it before placing animal pictures onto butcher paper.

Grasslands: soil, grass, dry, sunny, mudholes
Temperate Forests: moist, streams, lakes, rivers, trees
Tropical Forests: hot, muggy, moist, vines, rain, waterfalls, palm trees
Desert: dry, hot, sunny, dirt, windy, sandy, mirage
Polar: icy, snow, sunny, iceberg, cold, oceans

Suggested Activities *(cont.)*

Zoo Animals' Favorite Foods

Make a chart listing everyone's favorite food in the class. Ask them if they would like to eat grass, spiders, and roots everyday! Explain that these are some animals' favorite foods! Reread *Dear Zoo* and as you open each animal's container tell them the animal's favorite foods (refer to chart on page 40). Ask why the animals don't eat pizza and ice cream like we do. Explain that the zoo keeper fixes the animals' favorite foods for them because they are not in their real (natural) habitats. The zoo keeper makes sure that the animals have plenty of food and lots of water. Animals need water like we do to stay alive.

Explain that animals use different body parts to help them find and eat their food:

ears=hears	**mouth/teeth= ripping, chewing**
claws= ripping, tearing	**beak= pecking**
eyes= see	**trunk= grabbing, drinking**
nose= sniffing, digging	**webbed feet= chasing, digging in mud, swimming**

What do human beings use to help them get, eat, and enjoy their food?

Complete the worksheet on page 47 together or in small groups.

Additional Activities

Camouflage

Ask students how they stay safe?
Can what we wear keep us safe?

Animals "wear" special clothes (skin, feather, fur) to keep them safe. When you look at an animal's habitat and can't see the animal because it seems like it is hiding (but it is really there!), this is called camouflage. Camouflage keeps the animal safe. Review that some animals do not live in a safe place (like a lion's den), they live out in the open. By "blending" in they are safe from other animals that want to hurt them. Complete the worksheet on page 44 together. Then do the art activity on pages 45 and 46 as a total group or in small groups.

Have students try to camouflage themselves with their surroundings. (A boy wearing a red shirt can "blend in" with a red door.)

Suggested Activities *(cont.)*

Additional Activities *(cont.)*

- **Giraffe Fun:** Make the giraffe puppet on pages 48 and 49. Use to encourage oral language. Tell the students to place their giraffes under, over, in, behind, next to different items in the classroom.

  Use the giraffe as a pattern. Trace the giraffe 11 times. Create a math game. Back the copies with oaktag for sturdiness. Do not put the spots on the giraffes' necks yet. Place no spots on one neck, one spot on the next, and so on until you have ten spots on the last giraffe. Take 11 clothespins and place the numbers 0-10 on the pins. Put giraffe and clothespins in a knapsack and place in a center area. For center or free time have students match the numbers on the clothespins with the correct "neck."

- **Monkey See, Monkey Write:** Use page 50 for an excellent writing experience!

- **Zoo Mural:** Make a zoo mural for the hallway. Have students draw animals on large butcher paper. Place a second sheet of paper behind drawing and cut around shape. Staple along edges, leaving an opening to stuff animal with newspaper. Staple opening. Place the 3-D animals on a natural habitat background or in a more conventional zoo scene (cages).

- **Describe It!** *Dear Zoo* is an excellent resource for teaching describing words. Use the worksheet pages 53-55 as a group and complete by reading the description on each animal's container.

- **Long/Short:** Look at pictures of animals and notice the length of their tails. Make a chart listing animals with long and short tails. This can also be adapted to other animal body parts!

- **Dear Zoo Keeper:** As a class, write a letter to the local zoo keeper. Ask him which animal at the zoo would make the best class pet.

- **Going on a Zoo Hunt:** Using rope or masking tape, create a pathway around the classroom or on the playground. Play a rhythmic beat on a drum and have the students follow the rhythm as they go exploring for animals in the different land regions.

42   © 1990 Teacher Created Materials, Inc.

Suggested Activities *(cont.)*

Additional Activities *(cont.)*

Endangered Animals: Explain that some animals are not able to have lots of babies because they are being killed, or their land region is being destroyed. When this happens, the animal is called endangered. Decide on one endangered animal that your class can learn about. Make buttons to let everyone know you want to save that animal. (Buttons are circles of colored construction paper pinned to the student's clothing.)

A Safari Adventure: As a class make Zoorific Granola on page 73. Place 1/2 cup of granola into a small plastic bag for each student. Explain that the class will be going on a Safari Adventure to look for wild animals. Walk together through a "prepared" room (either stuffed animals or pictures of animals have been hidden around room). Students will enjoy discovering where the "camouflaged" animals are hiding! After all the hard hiking, students sit down and enjoy their bags of granola and a cup of fruit punch or other drink.

CULMINATING ACTIVITY

A Trip to the Zoo

Plan a day to take the class to the zoo. Use the field trip form on page 56. Try to have one adult guardian for every four children. Sometimes the zoo will send a representative out to speak to your class before going on the field trip. After the zoo experience, write a group big book of what the class saw and enjoyed at the zoo. Display.

Hidden Animals

Find and color the hidden animals.

Camouflage Snake

Directions:

1. Cut a sponge into 1 1/2"/4 cm squares.
2. Pour three or four colors of tempera paint in a small dish. Do not mix!
3. Dab sponge in paints so sponge looks multicolored.
4. Dab over snake (p. 45) and rocks (p. 46) until completely covered. Let dry.
5. Cut out snake and paste between rocks. Can you still find him?

Name _____ **Date**_____

Camouflage

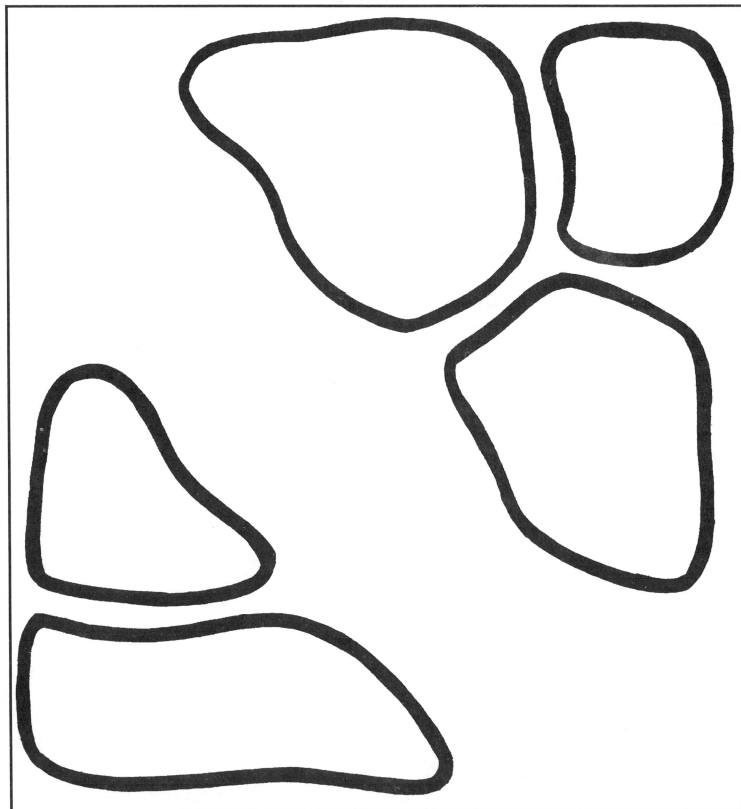

Name _____

Feed the Zoo Animals

- -

Cut and paste next to the right animal.

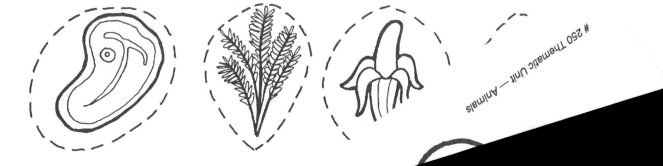

250 Thematic Unit—Animals

© 1990 Teacher Created Materials, Inc.

Giraffe Puppet

1. Color giraffe.
2. Cut out.
3. Glue onto small paper bag to make a puppet.

*See page 42 for suggested activities.

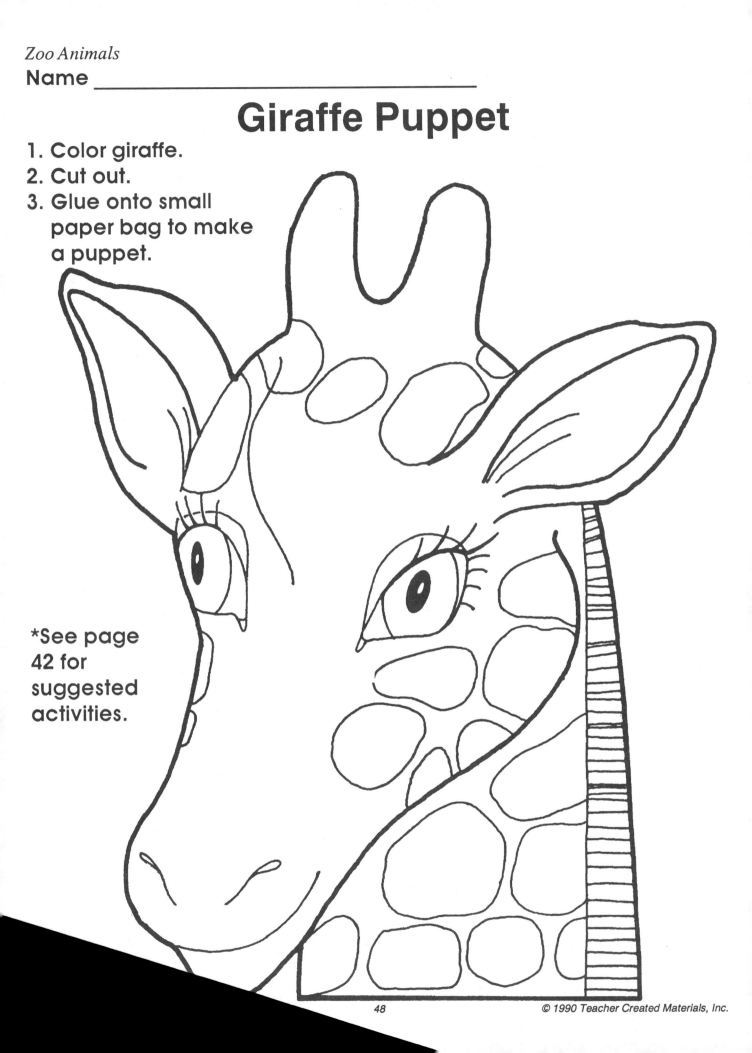

© 1990 Teacher Created Materials, Inc.

Giraffe Puppet *(cont.)*

*See page 42 for suggested activities.

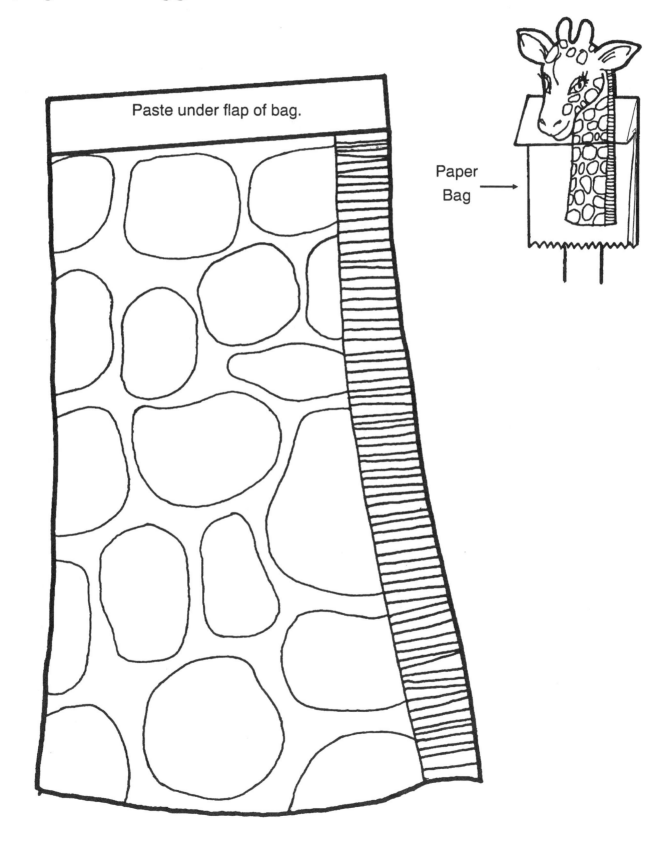

Paste under flap of bag.

Paper Bag →

Monkey See, Monkey Write

The following activity can be used for a handwriting experience (copying the poem), or for an open-ended writing experience.

Preparation

Copy the monkey head on page 78, one per student.

Read a supplemental story to the class about monkeys (*Curious George* or *Caps for Sale,* for example).

Activity

1. Hand out monkey pattern to each student. Allow them to color and cut it out. (For younger students, a parent helper or aide may do the cutting.)

2. Paste the edge of the monkey's head under the edge of an 18" X 12"/45 cm x 30 cm piece of construction paper. Place a smaller sheet of writing paper with lines in the middle of the construction paper. Staple or paste in place. Students may wish to add the monkey's hands and tail.

3. Have students copy poem below, write a summary of the story you read to them, or write a monkey story of their own on the paper. Display the finished monkey writing.

Monkey, Monkey,

Swinging on a vine,

Come down

for a banana,

So I can make

you mine!

George was
a funny monkey.
He got away.
He went to
the zoo.
He got in trouble!
I like George.
By Denise

Name _____   **Date** _____

Match the Zoo Animals

Cut and paste. Color.

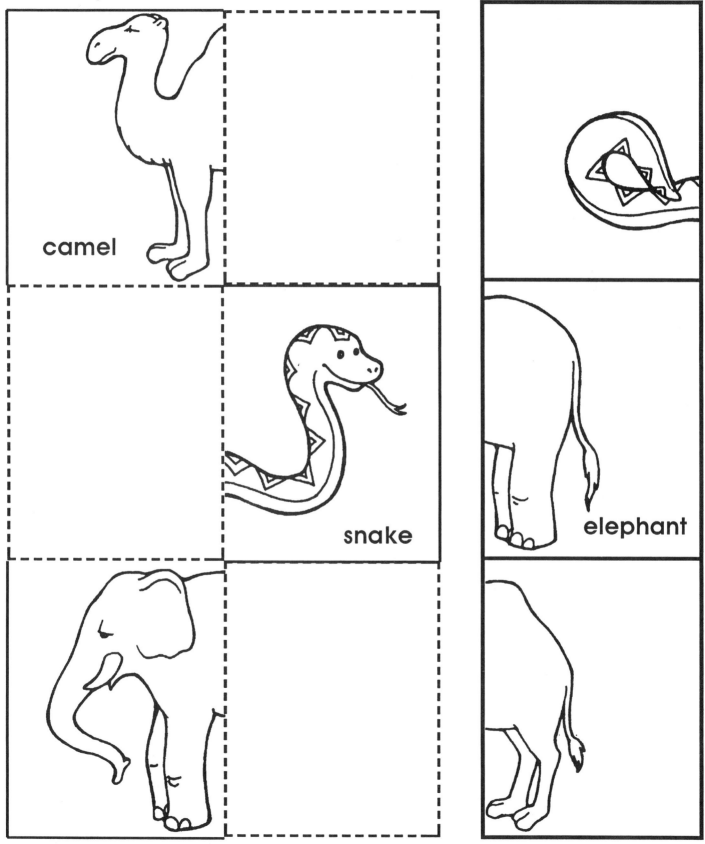

camel

snake

elephant

© 1990 Teacher Created Materials, Inc.

Name _____ **Date**_____

Zoo Puppets

1. Color zoo puppet faces.
2. Cut and paste on painted tube.
3. Add a tail.

"Dear Zoo" Flap Book

1. Color pages 53-55.
2. Cut out the containers on page 53.
3. Glue the container doors to pages 54 and 55.
4. Make a cover, fold, and staple for a flap book.

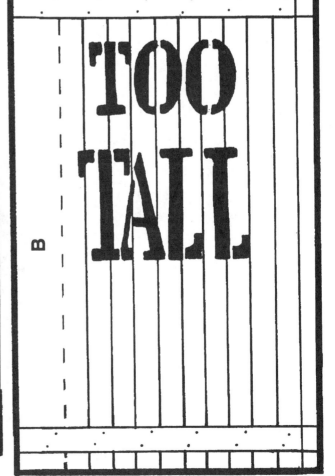

"*Dear Zoo*" Flap Book *(cont.)*

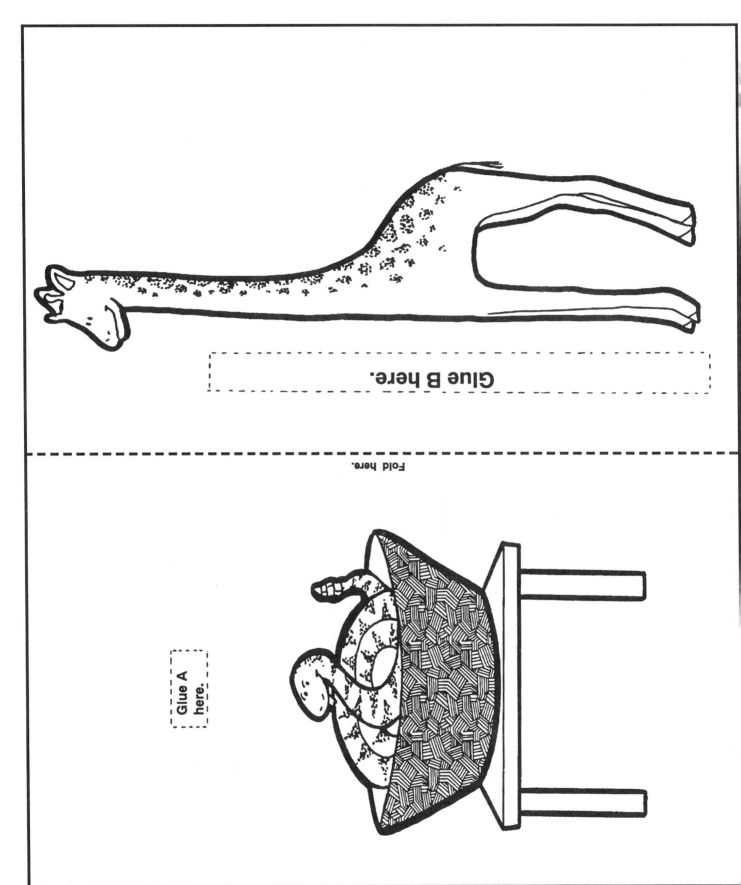

Glue B here.

Fold here.

Glue A here.

"Dear Zoo" **Flap Book** *(cont.)*

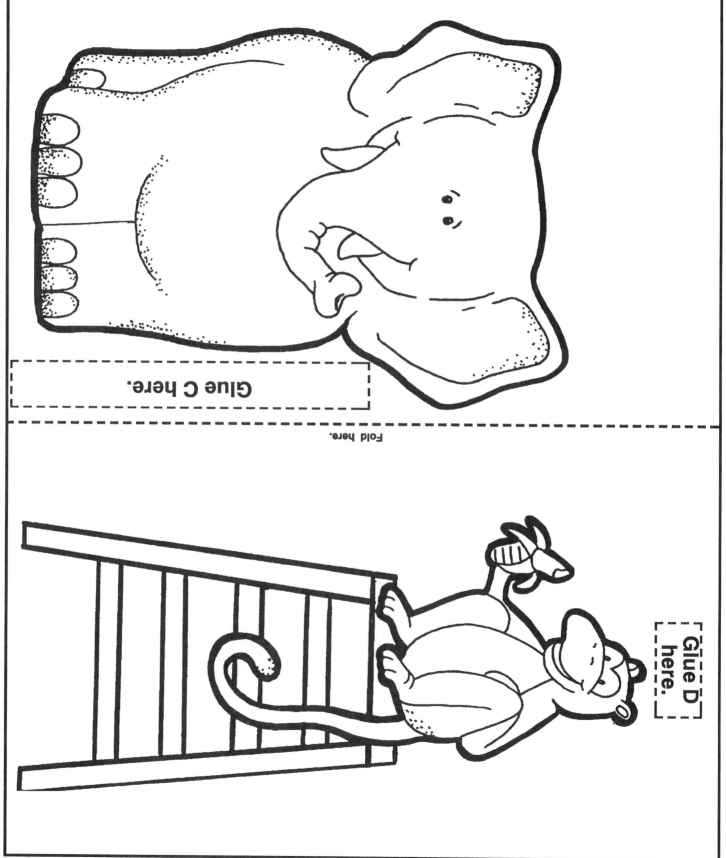

Glue C here.

Fold here.

Glue D here.

Field Trip Notice

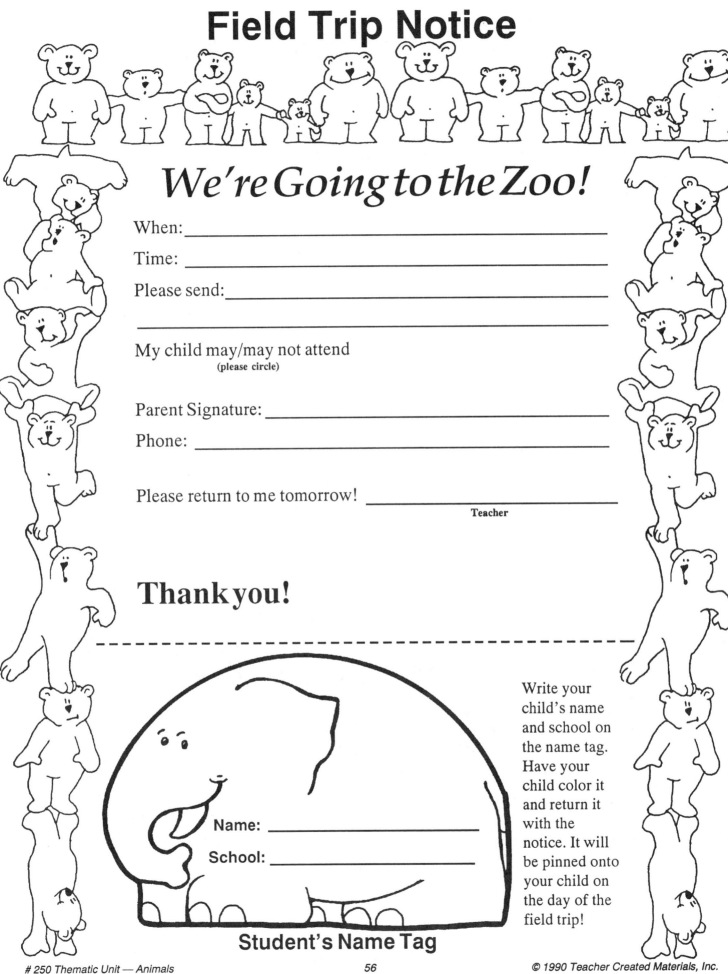

We're Going to the Zoo!

When: _____

Time: _____

Please send: _____

_____

My child may/may not attend
(please circle)

Parent Signature: _____

Phone: _____

Please return to me tomorrow! _____
                                    Teacher

Thank you!

- -

Name: _____

School: _____

Write your child's name and school on the name tag. Have your child color it and return it with the notice. It will be pinned onto your child on the day of the field trip!

Student's Name Tag

56

© 1990 Teacher Created Materials, Inc.

Pets

The Pop-Up Pet Shop

By Rod Campbell

Summary

It's time to go to the pet shop and choose a pet! Enjoy looking at a puppy, kitten, goldfish, rabbit, hamster, and bird. Each page describes the pet and contains a pop-up action feature. On the last page the students will delight in guessing the pet chosen to go to a new home!

Suggested Activities

Concepts

A. Some animals are tame; some are wild.

B. Pets need shelter, food, water, exercise...and love.

Concept Activities

Pets Are Tame

Show pictures of wild animals (tiger, hippo, rhino). Ask why these animals would not make good pets. (Try to gear answers to, "They will hurt you.") Animals that are not used to people, or animals that can hurt you, are called wild animals. Animals that like people and will not hurt them are called tame animals.

Make a list of everyone's pet. Include the type and name of each pet. Ask if their pets are tame or wild. Why?

On large chart paper, make a graph showing the students' pets. Give a square self-sticking note (one per pet) to each student. Have them draw a little picture of their pet. (If they have no pet, have them draw a pet they'd like.) Let them come to the graph and place their picture in the appropriate space. When completed, read the graph. See which animal is in the most homes, which is in the least, how many homes have no pet, etc.

Look in magazines for examples of wild and tame animals. Cut and paste on chart paper. Display.

Play "Tame Pet Riddles." Always start with the statement, "I am tame." Then describe a common household pet.

Examples:

I am tame. I am furry. I live in a cage.

I get exercise in a little wheel. What am I? Hamster

I am tame. I fetch the paper. I have four legs and a tail. I can bark. What am I? A dog

Suggested Activities *(cont.)*

Concept Activities *(cont.)*

What Our Pets Need

To stay safe and healthy we need: food, water, shelter, exercise...and love. Pets need the same things, too!

Explain each need in detail. Have students give examples of the foods they feed their animals and the ways in which they exercise their pets.

Explain that shelter means the pet's "house." Complete page 62 together or in small groups.

Review concepts by showing a stuffed dog, a leash, a water bowl, a doggie dish, a can of dog food, and chewy treats. Ask students what each item has to do with keeping the dog safe and healthy.

Have students make the happy, healthy dog on pages 63 and 64. Provide 18 X 11"/45 x 27 cm sheets of colored paper. Have students paste dog to paper and draw the five needs of a pet. Have them write or dictate a sentence or two about their happy, healthy dog!

For an across-the-curriculum activity let students put sight words, ABC letters, or math numbers on the body of the dog for practice and review. Or, write care-of-pet words on the dog and use to write a Big Book or accordion book about pets. (The dog's body could be folded to form an accordion book.) Read and display.

Additional Pet Activities

Pet Day: Assign a day and time for each student to bring in a living pet from their home. Make sure the student's parent (or other responsible adult) brings in the pet at the set time and takes it home after the child gets to share their pet with the class. If a camera is available, take a picture of the child with his/her pet. After students have brought in their pets, display the photos for all to see! If pets are not allowed at your school, students can bring in a picture of their pet and share it with the class.

Pet Rocks: Let the students choose some rocks from the playground to create a "pet" rock. After painting the rocks, little craft eyes and a red felt tongue may be added. Put the pet rocks at a free time touching table. Have students hold the pet rocks to see which are heavy and which are light. They can also classify the pet rocks by their weight.

 © 1990 Teacher Created Materials, Inc.

Suggested Activities *(cont.)*

Additional Pet Activities *(cont.)*

Cause and Effect: This is a very difficult concept for young students. Using page 65, explain that when we do something (cause), a new event (effect) will happen. Complete the worksheet together or in small groups.

Pet Parade and Writing Project: Hand out page 66, along with various sizes of colored paper, crayons, chalk, markers, feathers, and yarn. Have students draw and decorate the outline to look like their favorite kind of pet. Cut out the animal and paste onto heavy tagboard.

Staple a tongue depressor near bottom, so student can hold easily. Go on a marching pet parade around the classroom or school. Play music on a portable cassette player, encouraging children to stay in step to the beat of the music. When the parade is finished, have students sit on floor with their created pets and write a class Big Book about their parading experience! Display.

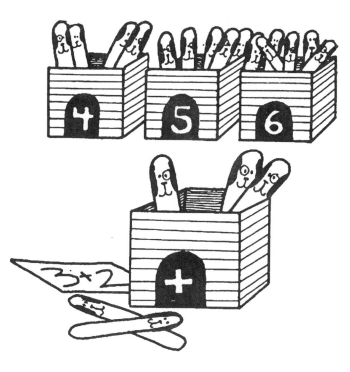

Mouserific Math: Explain that some people keep mice as pets. Read a mouse story, such as *If You Give A Mouse A Cookie* to the class. Discuss the foods that mice like to eat, emphasizing cheese. Hand out page 67 and have students complete after explaining the directions.

In the Dog House: To practice counting, turn children's small milk cartons into dog houses and turn craft sticks into dogs. Write the numbers 0-10 on "dog houses." While students are at a center or during free-time, allow them to put the correct number of dogs into each dog house.

Extension: Use only one dog house and provide simple addition problems. Have students put the number of dogs in the problem into the dog house as they work the problem. Place the correct answer on the back of the card so that the students can self-check their answers.

Suggested Activities *(cont.)*

Additional Pet Activities *(cont.)*

My Pet Counting Book: Using pages 68 and 69, have students create their own number book.

Rabbit Food! Some people own a rabbit as a pet. The care and feeding of a rabbit is the same as with a dog or a cat. Show a picture of a rabbit. Use the picture to review animal body parts. Ask the students what the five needs of the rabbit are (water, food, exercise, shelter, and love). Say that you would like to give them each a fuzzy rabbit to take home, but instead you'll do the next best thing! Make a tasty funny–bunny nutritional treat for everyone to eat. Have the ingredients ready to make Rabbit Salad (page 72). "Build" the rabbit in sequential order, encouraging students to follow directions carefully. This may be done in a total or small group setting. When the rabbits are finished, take a picture with an instant camera and give to each child as a memento of their "pet" rabbits.

Scrub-A-Dub-Dub: Some pets need to be groomed (brushed) daily and bathed weekly. Ask why we, as humans, need to stay clean. Pets need to stay clean, too, especially if they are living in our homes. We don't want to get sick from germs or dirt that our pets might have on them. Send a note home explaining to the parents that the students are learning about caring for pets. Ask if they could please help out by allowing their child to wash and groom their own pet (or a relative or neighbor's pet). Ask them to help their child draw a picture of the bathing and/or brushing of the pet. When the student brings in the picture (and a sentence or two about the experience if capable of writing), post the picture on a bulletin board and present the student with a special "I-Took-Care-Of-A-Pet" cookie (recipe on page 73).

Check These Out! For additional activities and resources, look at pages 71 and 80. If your class has shown a special interest in a specific animal, consider expanding your animal unit by a week or two to teach your students more about that animal.

© 1990 Teacher Created Materials, Inc.

Culminating Activity

Stuffed Animal Day!

Use the Stuffed Animal Day Notice on page 70 to encourage all students to bring in a stuffed animal, the more unusual, the better. (You may wish to have extras on hand for those who are not able to bring one.) When this special day finally arrives, complete one or more of the following activities:

1. Call each student up to the front of the class and allow him to talk about his stuffed animal. When finished sharing, award him with an Animal Lover Award (see below).

2. Have another parade, but this time call it "An Animal Awareness Parade" and go into other classrooms in the school. Once inside a classroom, have one of your students explain how to take care of a pet.

3. During rest or nap time, allow the stuffed animals to take a quiet break, too!

4. Have each student write or dictate a story about her favorite stuffed animal, then draw a picture of it. Display both the story and the picture.

5. Classify everyone's animals by animal species, size, color, characteristics.

6. Review, or introduce, the concept that all names start with a capital letter. Write the "pet" name of each stuffed animal on chart paper. Display.

7. Put all the animals in alphabetical order by the species of the animal. (Example: Anteater, Bear, Cat...)

8. Count the number of stuffed animals by ones and by tens.

9. Take a class picture of everyone with their favorite stuffed animal. Develop and display!

Animal Lover Award

SEAL OF APPROVAL

_____
(student's name)

knows how to love and care for our animal friends!

_____
Date

_____
Teacher

Pet Houses

2. Cut.
3. Glue the pet to its house.

62

© 1990 Teacher Created Materials, Inc.

A Happy, Healthy Dog

1. Color pages 63-64.
2. Cut out.
3. Glue front of dog to Tab B.
4. Attach tail at O with a paper fastener.

*See page 58 for suggested activity.

A Happy, Healthy Dog *(cont.)*

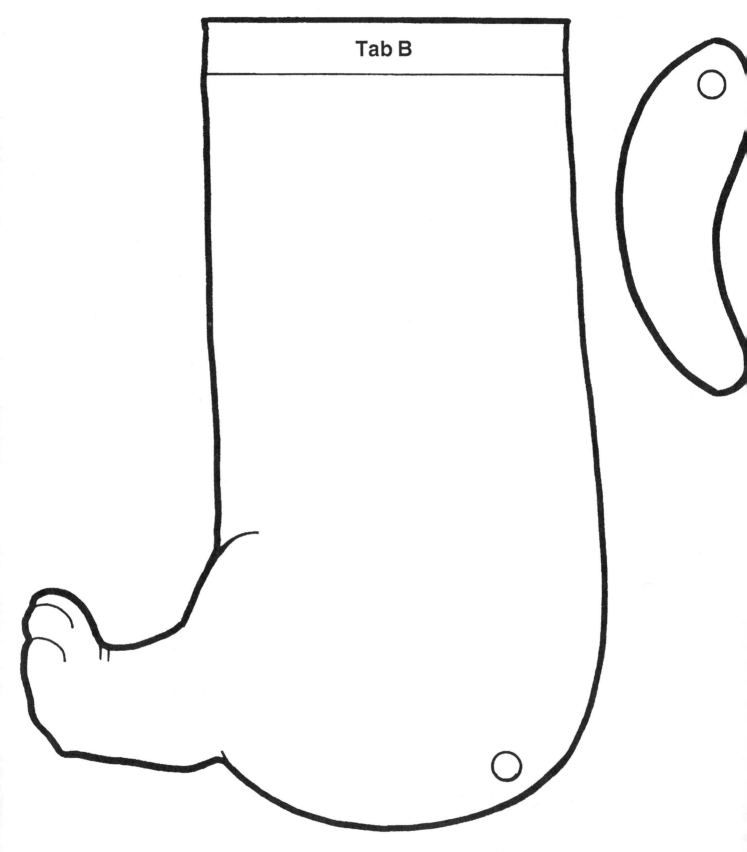

Tab B

64

© 1990 Teacher Created Materials, Inc.

Name_____

What Will Happen Next?

Color, cut, and paste.

Name _____

What Kind of Pet Will It Be?

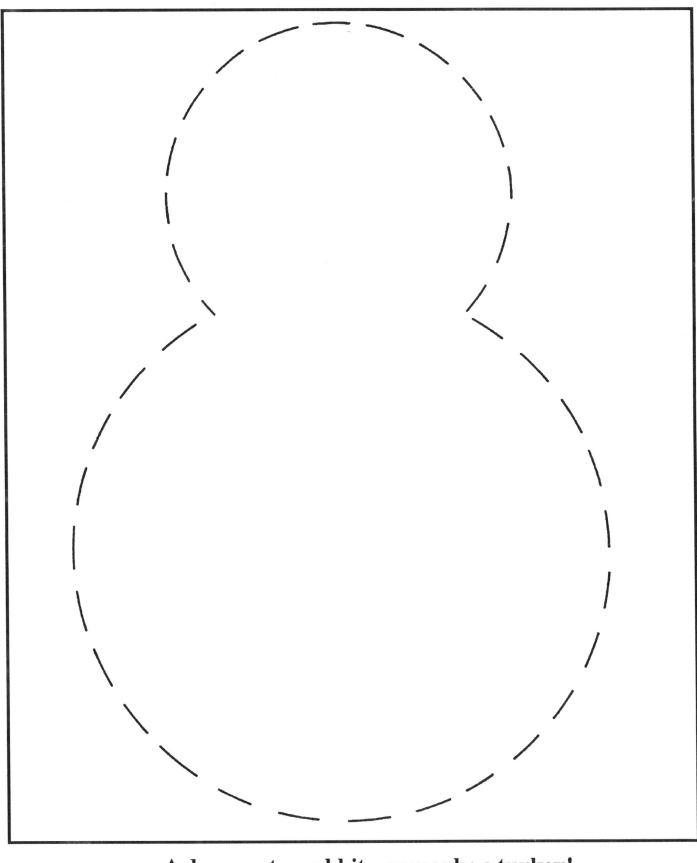

A dog, a cat, a rabbit...or maybe a turkey!

 © 1990 Teacher Created Materials, Inc.

Name_____

Mouse Fingers

1. Color.
2. Count the holes.
3. Count the mice fingers.

4. Cut out mice.
5. Put on correct wedge of cheese.

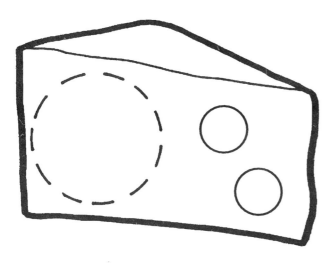

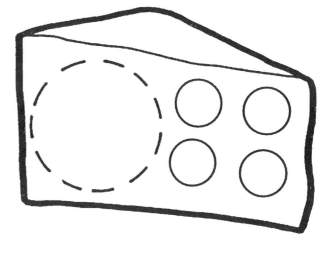

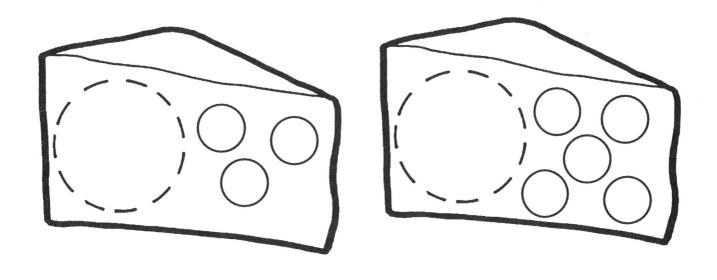

Counting Book

1. _____ the animals.
2. W____ ___ number of animals.
3. Color the animals.

4. Cut the pages apart.
5. Staple together to make a counting book.

68

© 1990 Teacher Created Materials, Inc.

Counting Book (cont.)

Pets Name

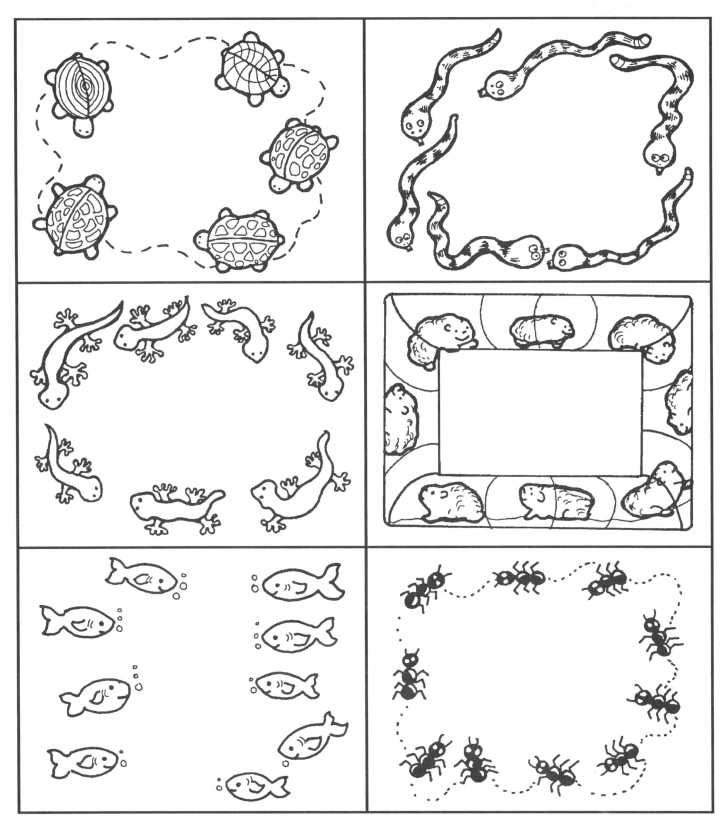

© 1990 Teacher Created Materials, Inc.

Stuffed Animal Day Notice

Stuffed Animal Day!

Please send me to school tomorrow with a stuffed animal. We are going to have lots of fun!

Unusual animals very welcome.

© *1990 Teacher Created Materials, Inc.*

General Animal Activities

- **Bulletin Board:** Make bulletin board display (pages 74-79) to introduce animal unit.

- **Animal Counting:** Use small plastic animals to practice counting, making sets, or working simple addition or subtraction problems.

- **Animal Alphabet:** Find a picture of an animal to represent each letter of the alphabet. Introduce or review each letter and its beginning sound. Post the pictures on the wall as you complete each letter. Keep posted for later reference and review.

- **Hoppers:** Make hopping animals by attaching strips of accordion-pleated paper to the back of a student-drawn picture.

- **Bird Feeders:** Make bird feeders by spreading peanut butter around a pinecone and roll in bird seed. Tie a string to the pinecone and hang outside the classroom window.

- **Animal Life Cycles:** For older students, introduce the concept of life cycles (example: frogs, butterflies).

- **Ant Farm:** Bring in an ant farm for the students to assemble and observe.

- **Where Animals Live:** Divide paper as shown at left. Provide magazines and have students find pictures of animals that live under ground, in the water, on the land, and above ground. Cut and paste onto background. Display.

- **Animal P.E.:** For fun physical education activities play Leap Frog, Duck-Duck-Goose, Red Rover.

- **Under the Microscope:** Using a child's microscope let each child have a turn looking at animal skin, hair, and feathers through the viewer. Discuss what each one looks like.

- **Animal Crackers:** Use animal crackers for a counting experience or to review oral language. (Example: Put the tiger cracker under your hand.) Then let students gobble up their counters!

- **Animal Puzzlers:** Make self-checking puzzles by cutting pictures of animals into four or six sections. Divide a game board (with the same dimension as the picture) into four or six spaces. Place corresponding information on the blank squares and back of corresponding picture piece. Students work puzzle by matching the given information. If done correctly, the student will be able to see a completed picture!

Recipes

Farm Scene Sandwiches

Ingredients:

1 slice wheat bread per student

1 square piece luncheon meat per student

1 square piece of cheese per 2 students

butter

Directions:

1. Spread butter onto the bread.

2. Place a slice of luncheon meat onto each slice of bread.

3. With farm animal-shaped cookie cutters, allow students to press a cookie cutter shape into one slice of cheese.

4. Place the cut out shape onto one slice of bread, and the outside (silhouette) shape on a second slice of bread. This will feed two students.

5. Repeat with remaining cheese slices until all students have a farm scene sandwich.

Enjoy sandwiches while listening to "Old McDonald Had a Farm" or other favorite musical tunes!

Note: Can be adapted to any animal category (zoo, circus, pet).

Rabbit Salad

Ingredients for each rabbit:

1 canned pear half

2 raisins

1 cinnamon candy

2 blanched almond slices

1 tablespoon (15 ml) cottage cheese

Directions:

1. Place pear half in the center of a sturdy paper plate.

2. At the smaller end create the face: nose–cinnamon candy; eyes–raisins; ears–almond slices.

3. At rounded end, place the spoonful of cottage cheese.

4. Eat and enjoy!

Optional: Line plate with a lettuce leaf before adding the pear.

72 © 1990 Teacher Created Materials, Inc.

Recipes

Zoorific Crunchy Granola

4 cups (1 L) old-fashioned rolled oats

1 1/2 cups (375 mL) flaked coconut

1 cup (250 mL) chopped pecans

1/2 cup (125 mL) unsalted sunflower seeds

1/2 cup (125 mL) wheat germ

1/2 cup (125 mL) firmly packed brown sugar

2 teaspoons (10 mL) cinnamon

1/2 cup (125 mL) vegetable oil

1/2 cup (125 mL) water

3 tablespoons (45 mL) honey

1 teaspoon (5 mL) vanilla

1 cup (250 mL) raisins

1 cup (250 mL) chopped dates

Combine the first seven ingredients in a large bowl. Set aside. Stir together oil, water, honey, and vanilla in separate bowl until well–blended. Pour the oil mixture over the oat mixture and stir well. Spread mixture evenly onto 1 or 2 lightly greased jelly roll pans. Bake in preheated 300°F/170°C oven for 1 hour, stirring every 15 minutes. Bake until granola is lightly browned. Cool on pans on a wire rack. Stir in raisins and dates. Store in airtight containers.

I-Took-Care-Of-A-Pet Sugar Cookies

1/2 cup (125 mL) shortening

1 cup (250 mL) sugar

2 well-beaten eggs

1 tablespoon (15 mL) milk

2 1/2 cups (625 mL) sifted flour

1/2 teaspoon (2 mL) baking powder

3/4 teaspoon (3 mL) nutmeg

powdered sugar

Cream together shortening and sugar. Beat until light and fluffy. Add eggs and milk. Beat well. Sift together dry ingredients and add to shortening mixture. Mix well, shaping dough into a round ball. Wrap in wax paper and refrigerate for at least three hours.

Roll out on counter or board dusted with powdered sugar until dough is 1/4 inch/6 mm thick. Make a pattern from cardboard by copying the pattern below. Place pattern onto dough and cut out dog bone shape with a knife. Transfer to lightly greased baking sheet. Bake at 375°F/190°C for about eight minutes, or until lighly browned. Remove and cool on baking sheet for one minute. Transfer to wire rack with a spatula. Cool completely.

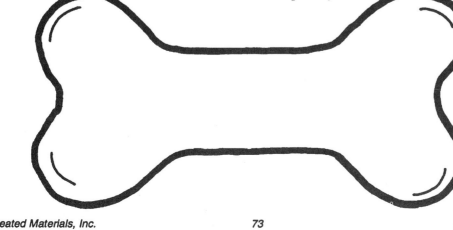

Bulletin Board

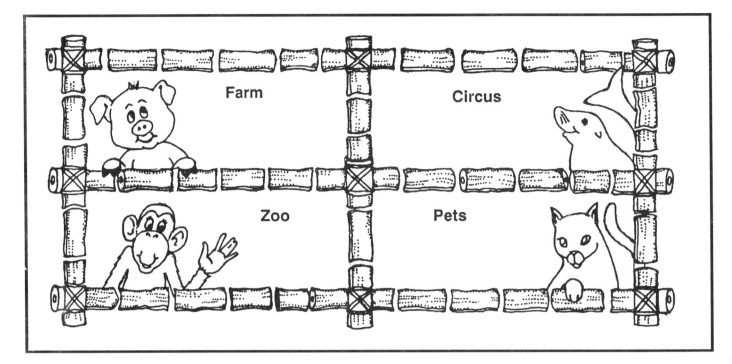

Objective

This bulletin board has been designed to display student's work as they learn about the four animal groups. As student's work is placed in the appropriate areas, it can be used to review information/skills taught.

Materials

Colored butcher paper (for background); brown construction paper (for bamboo borders); colored construction paper (for the pig, seal, monkey, and cat); scissors; tape or push pins; pre-made letters or markers (to create lettering)

Construction

1. Reproduce patterns (pages 75-79) onto appropriate paper and cut out.

2. Make lettering for title and headings.

3. Place butcher paper onto bulletin board for background.

4. Add bamboo borders, animals, and lettering.

Optional Uses

1. Reinforce/practice math number concepts by placing pictures of appropriate animals in each section and allow students to count them.

2. Put appropriate sight words in each animal section.

3. For a homework assignment, ask students to bring in a picture of an animal for each animal section. As they bring them in, let them classify them onto the bulletin board.

74

© 1990 Teacher Created Materials, Inc.

Bulletin Board *(cont.)*

Border piece (Lengths will vary depending on length/width of bulletin board used.)

Corner piece

(Make 4)

Center piece

(Make 5)

Bulletin Board *(cont.)*

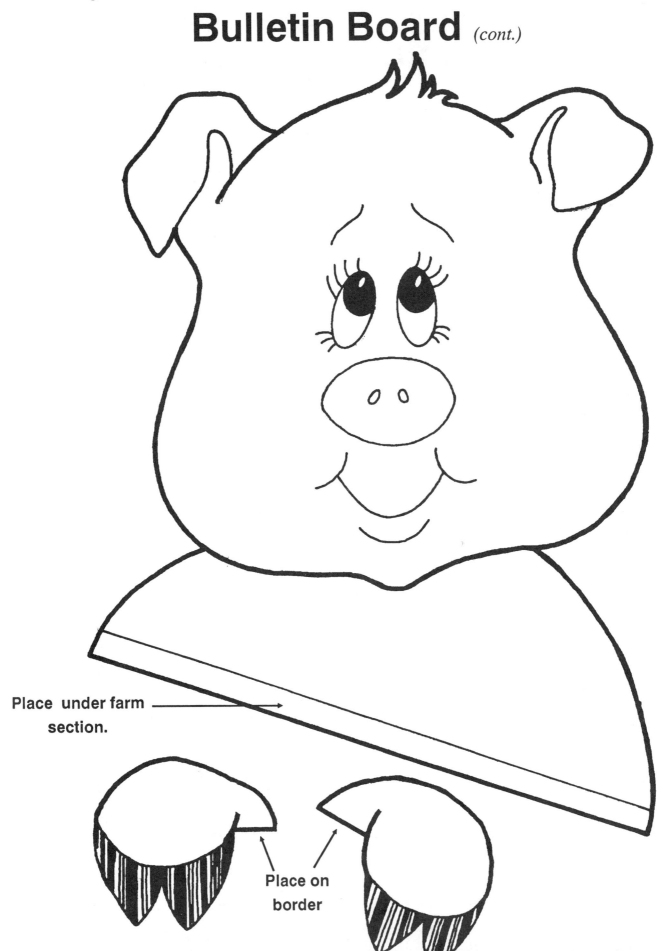

Place under farm section.

Place on border

Bulletin Board *(cont.)*

Place under border

Place under corner of circus section.

Bulletin Board *(cont.)*

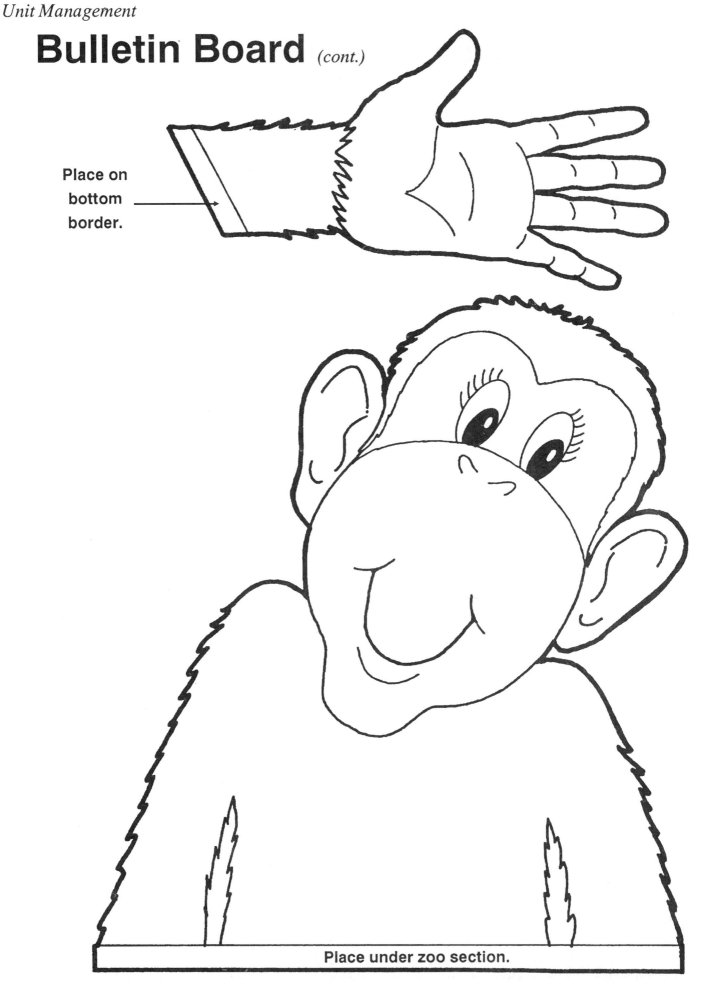

Place on bottom border.

Place under zoo section.

© *1990 Teacher Created Materials, Inc.*

Bulletin Board *(cont.)*

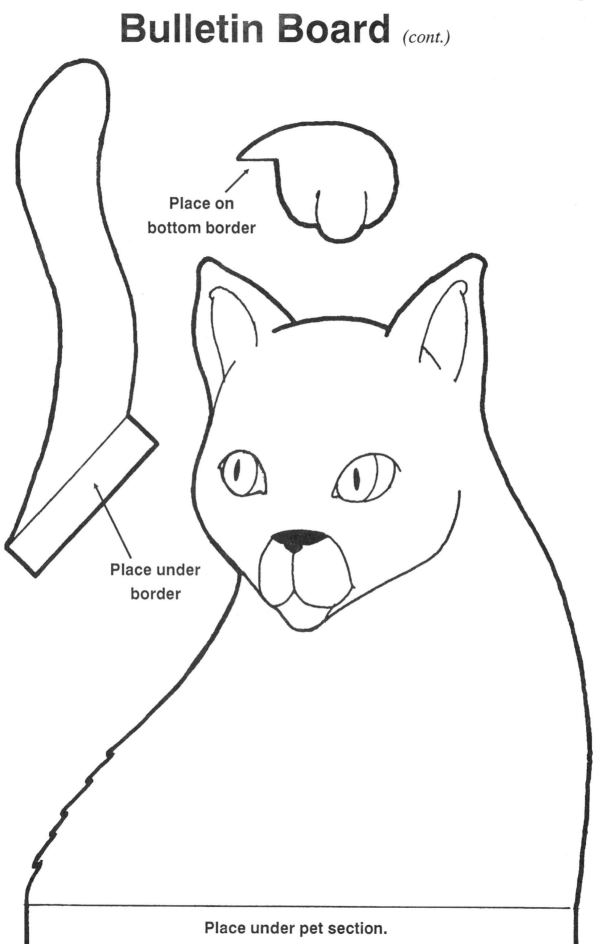

Place on
bottom border

Place under
border

Place under pet section.

Bibliography/ Resources

Suggested Books

Baker, Eugene. *Wild Animals*. Zachary's Workshop, 1989

Burningham, John. *Hey! Get Off My Train!* Crown, 1989

Campbell, Rod. *Dear Zoo*. Penguin,1987

Campbell, Rod. *The Pop-Up Pet Shop*. Macmillan Publishing, 1989

Demi. *Demi's Count the Animals One-Two-Three*. Putnam, 1986

Dunn, Phoebe. *Animal Friends*. Random House, 1985

Emberly, Rebecca. *Jungle Sounds*. Little, 1989

Hefter, Richard. *Pigs Think Pink*. Holt, 1978

Hill, Eric. *Spot Goes to the Farm*. Putnam, 1987

Hill, Eric. *Spot Goes to the Circus*. Putnam, 1986

Kherdian, David. *Animal ABC*. Random House, 1984

Moncure, Jane Belk. *Animal, Animal Where Do You Live?* Children's Press, 1975

Pearce Q.L and W.J. Pearce. *In the Barnyard (Nature's Footprints series)*. Silver Press, 1990

Penny, Malcolm. *Animal Camouflage*. Bookwright Press, 1988

Pfloog, Jan. *The Farm Book*. Golden Press, 1974

Pfloog, Jan. *The Zoo Book*. Golden Press, 1967

Ricciuti, Edward. *An Animal for Alan,* Harper and Row, 1970

Rojankovsky, Feodor. *The Great Big Wild Animal Book*. Golden Press, 1974

Ryden, Hope. *Wild Animals of America ABC*. Lodester Books, 1988

Snow, Pegeen. *A Pet for Pat*. Children's Press, 1984

Stobbs, William. *Animal Pictures*. Bodley Head, 1981

Taylor, Kate. *Animal Sounds*. Discovery Toys, 1988

Whitcombe, Bobbie. *Animals in Danger*. Brimax Books,1988

VCR Tapes

Bambi

Dumbo

Lady and the Tramp

Available through:

Walt Disney Home Video

Buena Vista Home Video, Burbank, CA 91521

Animals in the Wild

Baby Animals Just Want To Have Fun

Available through:

Scholastic's Animal Friends Video Series

Karl-Lorimar Home Video, Inc.

17942 Cowan,

Irvine, CA 92714